Highland
Steam

Highland Steam

A Scrapbook of Images from the Kyle, Mallaig and Highland Lines

Bill Williams

With a foreword by
John Barnes

Northern Books
from Famedram

Regular and not-so-regular visitors at Glenfinnan: above the service Sprinter on the Fort William-Mallaig run and below the Hogwarts Express on a rare filming mission.

Foreword
by John Barnes
Glenfinnan Station Museum

I FIRST became acquainted with Bill Williams and his Famedram/ Northern Books empire back in 1988 when researching material for the Centenary Exhibition planned by ScotRail to mark the start of construction of the West Highland Railway between Craigendoran and Fort William in 1889. I was also seeking publications and other sales items for Glenfinnan Station, where I had my own ideas for developing a West Highland Line museum in the soon-to-become redundant station buildings.

I was immediately impressed by Bill's infectious enthusiasm for all things pertaining to railways in the Highlands, and also for the architecture, history and culture of the area. His extensive range of publications was mind-boggling, especially when you realised that this was fundamentally a one-man show. I wish Bill every success with this new publication, which celebrates 25 years of steam activity on the railways of the Highlands.

His request for me to write this foreword is, he says, in recognition of the part I have played myself in keeping steam alive in the Highlands over the past 25 years. I have done my best, and certainly, in the crunch years of 1994 /95, when the future of steam to Mallaig, and the Fort William Sleeper seemed doomed, I was pleased to join in Bill's STORM protest (Stop this Railway Madness) and do what I could at a local level.

You only have to imagine what a sad and dejected place Fort William station would have been at 10 o'clock in the morning if the madness had been allowed to go ahead. Instead, for much of the year

Not a Mafia staff car but a sturdy snowplough, preserved by the Glenfinnan Station Museum

the welcoming sound of the bagpipes is now greeting the arrival of the sleeper from London and marking the departure of the Jacobite Steam Train, with the platforms teeming with up to 400 eager and happy rail riders.

Setting up the basis of a "new order" for the steam service was a role I was happy to provide: making contact with David Smith, the new owner of the Carnforth Lancashire Steamtown empire and the fledgling West Coast Railway Company, liaising with ScotRail and the local enterprise company, and helping to appoint key local operating personnel was an intensely satisfying achievement. I myself became involved in various capacities ranging from cleaner to guard and Train Manager.

As Vice-President of the Friends of the West Highland Lines, I was also able to campaign at a policy level for the recognition of heritage aspects and tourism as important parts of the future strategy for railways in the Highlands.

Through representation at the Highland Rail Partnership and by setting up the Highland Rail Heritage group, the various Friends organisation for all the Highland lines, successfully extended the range of steam train operations to include Oban, Aberdeen, Perth, Inverness, Kyle, Wick and Thurso.

My own overwhelming and abiding impression of the past 25 years has been that the dedication of a small number of devoted individuals, most of whom receive little recognition for their enormous effort, has secured the continuity of the steam product against seemingly insurmountable odds.

I've often pondered at their source of motivation. Is it all down to being "fired by steam"; "driven by steam"; "having steam in the blood;" "the lure of steam"; "the romance of steam"? Or simply "THE POWER OF STEAM"

This book may well help to throw some light on the phenomenon.

JOHN BARNES
Glenfinnan

MacPuff, kilted warrior dreamt up by the Highland Vigilantes to fight for the Highland lines

Introduction:
Save these Lines!

THIS IS not primarily intended as a book for the railway enthusiast (though perhaps some will cast an eye over it). It is an extended hymn of praise for what I, with many others, consider some of the most spectactular rail routes in the world. Its aim is to get this message across to a whole lot of readers worldwide who might not otherwise realise quite what they were missing and. most important of all, to keep these lines open.

I 'discovered' these magical lines while working as a hack in Glasgow back in the seventies. Miraculously, thanks in no small measure to some gutsy 'MacPuff' campaigning by the Highland Vigilantes (or Village Aunties as they were cruelly called) these Highland lines had escaped Dr Beeching's axe in the sixties, but rural rail lines with little potential for profit are never safe, whichever sort of Tory government (Labour or Conservative) is in power.

In those days. unbelievably, governments were prepared to close lines to unlock the scrap value in the rails. They were even prepared to do insane things like singling long stretches of important, previously double tracked lines to grub a bit of money from the scrap dealer. Long vital stretches of the Highland line from Perth to Inverness were vandalised in this way.

At the beginning of the seventies the Department of the Environment hit on the Kyle line, from Dingwall to Kyle of Lochalsh. Apparently, it was costing all of £318,000 a year in subsidy to keep the line going, while in fares it could only bring in a measly £51,000 – a thousand a week. Close it, said the Minister, but the locals thought otherwise amd put up a fight.

I remember being sent up to Plockton to interview the redoubtable Torquil Nicholson - the local councillor who was fronting the campaign to save the line from closure. I remember being completely dumbfounded when I got there, by a ciruitous route that included a trip on the old Strome ferry – now "No Ferry"). Close a beautiful scenic rail line like this? You must be joking?

At that time I was making the move from journalism into publishing.

British Railways Board
PUBLIC NOTICE

ansport Acts 1962-68

SENGER SERVICE
INVERNESS—KYLE OF LOCHALSH

d below is a letter from the Department of the Environment referring to the proposal to withdraw the rail passenger service between INVERNESS and KYLE OF LOCHALSH
consent to the withdrawal the Secretary of State for the Environment has stipulated that this should NOT take place before 1 JANUARY 1974

Department of the Environment
2 Marsham Street
LONDON SW1
21 December 1971

INVERNESS—KYLE OF LOCHALSH RAIL CLOSURE PROPOSAL

The late Councillor Torquil
Nicholson, Plockton, stout
defender of
the Kyle Line

In the Loch Lomondside village where I had set up shop as a country printer publisher lived the celebrated chronicler of the outdoors, Tom Weir.

As one of my very first publications (after Alexander Maclean's The Haggis, illustrated by a then almost unknown Mairi Hedderwick), I asked Tom if he would consider writing a brief campaigning history of the line with the aim of highlighting the insanity of destroying such a valuable tourist asset and in the process attracting more visitors to make the idyllic journey from Inverness, though Dingwall to Kyle of Lochalsh.

Tom obliged, supplying some of his memorable black and white photographs. It was a modest production, turned out on a glorified office duplicator, but it somehow caught the public imagination and enjoyed a very respectable sale, helped by the enthusiastic support of many along the line, from the Kyle Pharmacy in Kyle to the John Menzies (as it then was) station bookstall on Inverness station, via just about every business along the way.

In 1974 we won the first round and the plan to axe the Kyle line was officially dropped. But was the line really safe?

Certainly the trains continued to run and, most important of all, when the elements played their part and disrupted travel, often by seriously damaging the track, it was eventually repaired. Early one morning in 1989 the handsome stone arches of the Ness Bridge, which carried the line north out of Inverness, collapsed and were washed away by the swollen river.

It could have been the perfect excuse to axe all rail services north of Inverness and replace them with buses. Miraculously this did not happen and within a year a sturdy new bridge opened and trains were able to run once more to Kyle and Wick and Thurso.

The next serious threat to the Highland's scenic rail routes came with the madcap plan to privatise the railways. This time it was the West Highland Line, to Fort William and on to Mallaig that seemed to be most seriously threatened. A big part of the attraction of rail travel to the West Highlands has always been the London-Fort William sleeper service, that miracle by which you went to bed in London and woke up on the shores of Loch Linnhe. (In reality you probably woke up many times on the way, but it was still a firm favourite with summer visitors and schoolboys of all ages.)

As part of the process of fattening up the goose to make it more attractive to market, little inconveniences like running a proper locomotive hauled train the length of the country had to be eliminated. The package on offer needed to be simple and easy to manage – like diesel engined railcars (the so-called Sprinter). Being effectively buses on rails they could, hey presto, be run by bus companies (and guess who now runs most if not all of them?).

So the Fort William sleeper would have to go. This seemed to me a mad and very bad idea so I booked a hall in Fort William and called a public meeting to protest the decision. The result was amazing. On a diabolical

Willing hands help with final positioning . Wyllie, with bunnet, is just to the left of the crane.

End of the line? The threatened Fort William sleeper about to plunge into Loch Linnhe.

winter night, such as only the West Highlands can produce, getting on for 300 brave folk turned out to hear speakers Brian Wilson and Charles Kennedy berate the ill-conceived plan.

We had obviously touched a raw nerve. An organisation, STORM (STOp this Railway Madness), was born and further protest meetings were held in other threatened centres such as Inverness, Kyle and Perth.

The public reaction was heartening, but to get national coverage we needed to get on the telly. This meant producing an arresting visual image that could be transmitted across the world. Solution? Call in the inspired installation artist and scul?tor George Wyllie.

With a budget of next to nothing in the bank George and I went round Fort William seeking practical help and support. The response once again was amazing. Everyone said yes. In the huge sawmill complex at Corpach – reputedly the largest in Europe – I was about 30 seconds into my pitch when the boss said, "Yep" "Tell us what you need". It was the same at the Roads Department. Talk about pushing at open doors.

George had won fame with his Straw Locomotive, suspended from one of the giant Clydeside cranes – an eloquent and painful reminder of a lost industrial past. A locomotive plunging into the loch seemed like a pretty appropriate image, but could it be done credibly on a budget of less than a thousand?

With George Wyllie on the job the answer was an emphatic yes. A powerful West Highland sun shone down on our efforts and at the end of an exhausting day George's creation was in place, tilting terrifyingly into Loch Linnhe from a strategic point at the entrance to the town.

The resulting coverage was astounding. Besides the local news, we made ITV's News at Ten, virtually every UK newspaper and many abroad.

With the efforts of many other agencies and individuals the battle was eventually won. The sleeper was saved, though in all honesty it was a much cut-down service that survived. All other loco hauled services, including the Explorer summer trains, so popular with Railcarding backpackers, and the splendid Motorail car carrying service had to go so that the mindless Sprinter regime could rule supreme.

In this depressing scenario there was one chink of light: it looked as though as well as the sleeper the summer steam train from Fort William to Mallaig would be safe. Steam had come back to the Mallaig line in 1984, the trail being blazed by a plucky run from Fort William to Arisaig by the venerable Maude.

This led to a regular summer service which has grown in popularity and professionalism over the years so that 25 years after it started it was well nigh impossible to get a seat without booking well in advance. It is a real credit to those involved in running this service that this has been achieved with virtually no recourse to public funding. The beneficial effects to the

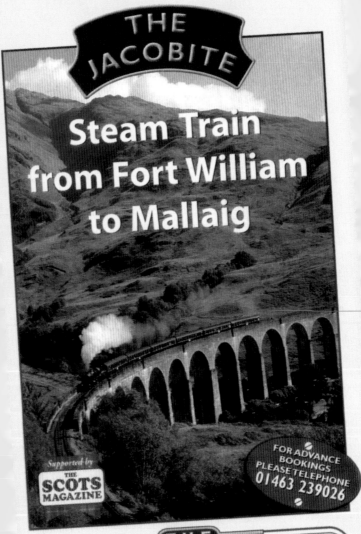

1901-2001 100 YEARS OF TRAINS TO MALLAIG

FOLLOW THE ROAD TO THE ISLES

THE JACOBITE

Steam Train from Fort William to Mallaig

FOR ADVANCE BOOKINGS PLEASE TELEPHONE 01463 239026

Supported by
THE SCOTS MAGAZINE

THE WEST COAST RAILWAY COMPANY LTD

18 June to 28 September 2001

Promotional leaflet for the Jacobite steam service for 2001 – the centenary of the line. Reproduced courtesy WCRC Ltd.

local tourist economy of this super popular visitor attraction must be truly immense.

Sadly the example set by the Jacobite operation has not been emulated on the other Highland lines. In many ways of course the Fort William - Mallaig run is the perfect model. Departure from Fort William at a civilised hour (just after the sleeper has arrived), an adventure stop at Glenfinnan and arrival in Mallaig just in time for a spot of lunch, or a wander around the shops and back to base in plenty of time for tea all makes for the perfect day out – the weather notwithstanding.

Maybe it is a little unrealistic to propose a regular steam day trip all the way from Inverness to Kyle and back. The timings could never be as user friendly as with the Fort William-Mallaig run. Inverness to Wick would be even more ambitious, but what about some less ambitious venture like Kyle to Strathcarron and back, or Inverness to Strathpeffer (yes, restore the spur from the main line) or even between Wick and Thurso?

Impossibly ambitious you may say, but probably nowhere near as costly as many of the ill-fated tourist schemes that have haemorrhaged money from the day they opened. (The list is too long to reprint here).

Sadly, though lip service is paid to its importance, tourist promotion still enjoys Cinderella status in Scotland with an endless series of inept initiatives thought up by politicians and administrators who would. most of them, struggle to run a whelk stall. Ah well, but that's another story.

T HE FOLLOWING pages recreate, in the first two sections, there-and-back steam journeys between Fort William and Mallaig and Inverness and Kyle. The third section records various steam outings to the north, south and east, radiating from Inverness. The final pages mark the departure down south of a recent, ambitious Great Britain wide special steam excursion.

As anyone who has set out to capture the wonder of steam in remote parts will know, there are plenty of obstacles to overcome – not the least of these being the weather, the usually very infrequent opportunities to film – and not forgetting the midgies! Given these difficulties, readers may be prepared to tolerate a lack of continuity that would give a film producer nightmares. One engine enters a tunnel and a completely different one comes out it of on a different day. We lurch without warning from 1984 to 2009, stopping at various years on the way, retracing our steps and moving on again.

But if we succeed in capturing some of the sheer glory of these lines then this might be counted success. If you do not already know this part of the world and its magical scenic railways come and see them for yourself – then tell all your friends. It really is a case of use them or lose them.

BILL WILLIAMS

Fort William from across Loch Linnhe

The 'new' Fort William station which replaced the old 'town' station

Approaching what was once Mallaig's railway pier, from the sea. The line now ends in the town

Fort William to Mallaig*
– 41 miles
(* *and back again*)

The rail journey from Fort William to the fishing and ferry port of Mallaig has been voted the most scenic in the world.

It is not, however, a summer only excursionist line, kept going solely as a tourist attraction. It is a working railway forming part of a valuable year-round link between Central Scotland, the southern part of Skye and in particular the charming Small Isles.

Built after an epic struggle against geography, the elements and financial hardship to capture the booming fish market, the line still performs a valuable social function throughout the year.

It is, though, in the summer that the line comes into its own. When regular steam excursions were introduced in the 1980s interest in the line soared and the day trip to Mallaig became one of Scotland's top tourist treats.

The photo sequence follows a variety of journeys either on special steam excursions or on the regular summer run, starting in the depot at Fort William, reaching Mallaig and then returning back to Fort William behind a number of different preserved steam locos.

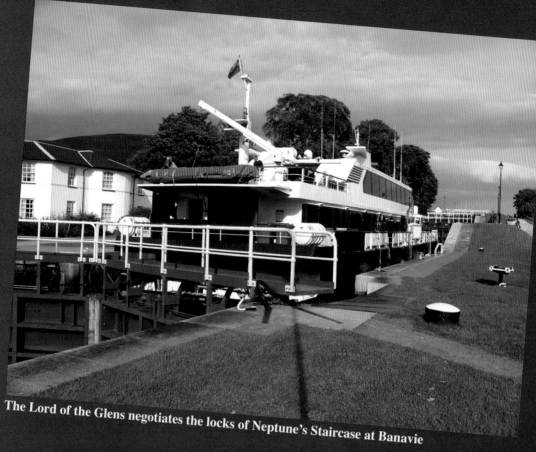

The Lord of the Glens negotiates the locks of Neptune's Staircase at Banavie

The preserved puffer VIC 32 moored at Corpach just beside the line

Restored dining car offering refreshment to visitors to the Glenfinnan Station Museum

Platform collection for your pcs

This way to the trains and more …

Bustling street scene outside Inverness town hall. The station is a couple of blocks to the left.

Kyle from across the water. The station-on-a-pier is to the left of the moored freighter, on th

Inverness to Kyle of Lochalsh*

82 miles
(* and back again)

Inverness to Kyle – or Kyle of Lochalsh to give it its true railway resonance – is a far more ambitious outing than Fort William to Mallaig. From Dingwall alone it is over 60 miles and winding around the Beauly Firth as the line does adds almost 20 miles or so from Inverness.

Just as with the Mallaig line it was a struggle to reach Kyle. Indeed at first they had to settle for Strome Ferry, some ten miles short of their final destination using an elaborate fleet of steamers to reach Skye and other island destinations.

The line finally arrived in Kyle in 1897 and, with the odd break for rock falls and landslides, has given sterling service ever since. In the war the line to Kyle (known as Port ZA) played a vital role transporting men and munitions. Today a lively Friends organisation maintains a busy interpretive centre and shop in part of the station.

The remains of the 1862 Ness bridge, swept away in 1989. The new bridge opened in 1990.

THE
NORTH BRITON

45407

26
D
SC

Iron road from Achnasheen to the Luib summit – the highest point on the line

The new Skye bridge, finally made toll free after a long campaign led by Robbie the Pict

Almost engulfed by timber, a Sprinter at Kyle station can just be seen in the background

Steaming past the oil rigs – a very rare steam excursion to the Far North at Invergordon

The summer's work over, locomotives and coaches cross the Clyde on their way back hom

Far North – South, East and West

O n the line to the Far North of Scotland the sight of a working steam engine is a very rare one indeed. Given the remoteness and the sparse population this is no surprise, so when it happens it is doubly remarkable.

In recemt decades it has taken an initiative like the Highland Rail Festival to bring the sound of steam to Caithness and Sutherland, and other northern, eastern and western parts have fared little better.

The pages that follow record some of the rarer outings to destinations such as Helmsdale in the North, and Taynuilt in the West. Also covered are the slightly more common journeys to the very heart of the Highlands – Inverness, with the odd diversion to Aberdeen and the East Coast thrown in for good measure.

The mighty Findhorn viaduct carries the line high above the river of the same name

The splendid corrugated Tomatin kirk, across the field from the Findhorn viaduct

The mighty 28 span Nairn masonry viaduct, longest in Scotland – opened in 1898

at Britain II, having crossed the Nairn viaduct, prepares for the descent to Inverness

The North Briton on the Nairn viaduct

The North Briton, 45407 and 60009, on the Nairn viaduct

Leaving Inverness

Approaching Helmsdale

Helmsdale

Leaving Helmsdale station

Passing Port Gower, south of Helmsdale

By Lothbeg Point, North of Brora

Standing at Brora

48151

GAUGE O GUILD

South from Brora

Approaching The Mound

Crossing Invershin viaduct

Fimdhorn viaduct – going south

By Loch Ericht, south of Dalwhinnie

Crossing the Tay (honest!) at Dalguise

On the Dubh Eas viaduct, north of Ardlui

North from Rannoch Station

Climbing above Auch towards the county march

At the county march north of Tyndrum

Tender first approaching Taynuilt

By Loch Awe in Argyll

Crossing the Deveron at Avochie by Huntly

Great Britain II passes through Inverurie

Aberdeen next stop

On Montrose's fine brick viaduct

On the home straight — Great Britain II passes Boddin going South